Original title:
Under the Green Umbrella

Copyright © 2025 Creative Arts Management OÜ
All rights reserved.

Author: Liam Sterling
ISBN HARDBACK: 978-1-80581-820-5
ISBN PAPERBACK: 978-1-80581-347-7
ISBN EBOOK: 978-1-80581-820-5

A Retreat in Emerald Abode

In a leafy nook, we hide,
Laughing as the raindrops slide.
Squirrels join our picnic feast,
While ants march on, not the least.

Lemonade spills on the grass,
Giggling at each clumsy pass.
A startled bird sings off-key,
Join our dance, oh, so carefree!

Glimmers of Sunlight Through Leaves

Sunbeams flicker, shadows play,
A butterfly flutters our way.
Here comes a bug with a hat,
No, wait, it's just my friend Pat!

Laughter echoes through the trees,
A raccoon steals our summer peas.
With watermelon seeds in tow,
We start a seed-spitting show!

The Soft Whisper of Greenery

Whispers rustle, soft and slow,
A leaf fell down — oh, what a blow!
A ladybug with flair so grand,
Wants to join our silly band.

Mossy seats, a comfy spot,
Finding treasures — who knew what?
A toad croaks jokes we can't resist,
Nature's stage, and we're the twist!

Solitude Beneath the Leaves

Secluded moments filled with cheer,
Monkeys swing and draw us near.
We balance snacks on our heads,
As twigs become our comfy beds.

Floating dreams on dandelion,
Hiccups laugh, they just won't align.
In this hideout, joy takes flight,
Emerald magic, pure delight!

Whispers of a Leafy Canopy

In the park where giggles bloom,
A squirrel's dance fills all the room.
Leaves wiggle like they've got a plan,
To drop acorns on a passing man.

Birds are plotting, quite sincere,
A mock debate, who's the best here?
The sun peeks through, a cheeky ray,
As laughter spills from kids at play.

Beneath the Verdant Shield

A picnic spread with sandwiches neat,
Was attacked by ants, now it's quite the feat.
A dog in shades lounges with flair,
While a cat judges from the nearby chair.

Pigeons strut as if they own,
This leafy stage, a feathered throne.
Who knew this shade held such a show?
Future comedians, all in tow!

Secrets of the Shaded Haven

Under the branches, a clown slipped by,
With a squeaky nose and a twinkly eye.
Children giggle, their secrets spill,
As ice cream drips down with a thrill.

The grass whispers stories of many a fall,
Tales of grand knights and brave grasshopper brawl.
All while the trees nod their heads in cheer,
As shadows dance, tickling the ear.

The Emerald Canopy's Embrace

Jellybeans tumble, a sweet little prank,
As giggling friends head off the plank.
A bug on a leaf, wearing a grin,
Plays hide and seek with a dog not too thin.

The air is thick with laughter and cheer,
While shadows play hopscotch, drawing near.
A twirling breeze whispers a joke,
As nature cracks up, beneath it broke.

A Canopy of Calm

A squirrel danced on a branch,
While bees practiced their jazz,
The rain had no chance,
For nature wears a feathered spazz.

Picnics planned with great delight,
Sandwiches take their flight,
The ants throw a party nearby,
All while we gaze at the sky.

A chubby dog steals a shoe,
As shadows stretch and bend,
We laugh at the sight anew,
In this leafy world, we're friends.

Beneath Foliage's Gentle Touch

A chipmunk sings a silly tune,
As shadows twist and play,
The light dances in a swoon,
While we nap the afternoon away.

Bright flowers peek through the greens,
With laughter in the air,
Nature's jokes are quite the scenes,
Waving their petals without a care.

A breeze tickles our noses,
We giggle, our spirits soar,
In this realm where anything goes,
We find joy in nature's lore.

The Leafy Dome of Dreams

With laughter drumming on the leaves,
A skunk wears a crown of flowers,
As we share our silly heaves,
In this humor-filled land of ours.

Bouncing frogs in a hopping race,
Chasing shadows left and right,
A butterfly steals the space,
As we cheer their fuzzy flight.

In a realm of funny sights,
Where laughter finds its way,
We dance with nature's light,
And let our worries sway.

Nature's Shelter Above

A raccoon runs a comedy club,
With jokes about the moon,
While we watch with a tiny snub,
And join in this merry tune.

Honeybees buzz with a twist,
Trying to sing and hum,
While we munch on fruit and tryst,
Nature's laughter is so fun.

The clouds join in with a grin,
Casting shadows on our glee,
In this world we spin, spin, spin,
With joy, we sip our iced tea.

Breeze Through the Verdant Realm

A squirrel in shades, quite the sight,
Rides a breeze, oh what a flight!
With acorns in hand and a grin so wide,
He dances on branches, a squirrel with pride.

The parrot shouts jokes, full of glee,
While bees hum tunes, buzzing in spree.
A ticklish tickle from the grass below,
Each giggle echoes, the trees put on a show.

The Essence of Nature's Embrace

The frog croaks riddles, witty and slick,
Jumping like a stand-up comic, oh what a trick!
With lily pads grinning, won't let him fall,
Each ribbit a punchline, entertainment for all.

A hedgehog in glasses reads books in the shade,
While mushrooms debate on the jokes they've made.
The sunbeams giggle, casting playful rays,
Nature's own laughter, brightening our days.

Harmony within Leafy Halls

The caterpillar hosts a tea party grand,
With ladybugs questioning, 'Can I lend a hand?'
Cupcakes of nectar and sandwiches green,
All sing in harmony, a quirky routine.

The trees sway gently, a waltz through the air,
And crickets play music, oh what a fair!
The snails spin tales of slow-rolling fun,
Each verse a twist, until day is done.

Hushed Moments in the Grove

A tiny mouse with a twit and a squeak,
Tells tales of cheese, it's quite the mystique!
With each little chuckle, the shadows dance,
A forest fiesta, oh what a chance!

The owls hoot echoes, wise yet absurd,
As they tell of the things they've unintentionally heard.
They nod at the sun, a bright yellow tease,
While chatting about clouds, floating with ease.

Sighs of the Shaded Realm

In a place where the leaves seem to giggle,
And sunbeams dance, oh so slyly,
Squirrels in suits play a grand game,
While birds drop nuts with a cheeky aim.

Beneath this dome of emerald cheer,
We chuckle at whispers that tickle the ear,
A frog on a log gives a comedic croak,
As shadows join in a mischievous joke.

The Canopy of Gentle Hues

A patchwork quilt of colors above,
Charmed by the antics, we laugh and shove,
The bugs do a ballet, legs all akimbo,
While rabbits perform their best disco.

With each fluttering leaf, a giggle escapes,
As gnomes in the shade plan their escape,
A turtle in shades takes a sip from a cup,
Sipping lemonade, he can't keep up!

Greenery's Gentle Enclosure

In an arena where daisies laugh loud,
A shy little frog leaps and bows to the crowd,
With each grand flourish, he slips and he lands,
Creating a puddle; oh how everyone stands!

The bumblebees buzz like a buzzing band,
While grasshoppers judge with a waving hand,
Here, in this realm of comical grace,
Nature's antics wear a silly face.

Harmonies in the Leafy Air

The branches sway, a waltz in the breeze,
A raccoon twirls with remarkable ease,
He trips on a vine, oh what a sight,
While crickets hum their tunes of delight.

In this green orchestra, laughter is shared,
With friendly fireflies, a show well-prepared,
As shadows grow longer, the giggles ignite,
A symphony born under the soft light.

The Sylvan Sanctuary

In a leafy nook where squirrels chatter,
A frog wearing glasses says, "It don't matter!"
The sun peeks through with a grin so wide,
While ants march in line, they take it in stride.

Beneath a big oak, a party takes flight,
With mushrooms as chairs, it feels just right.
The rabbits bring snacks, with carrots galore,
While the tortoise dances, though he's quite a bore.

A parrot recites Shakespeare with flair,
The deer roll their eyes, just not quite a pair.
"Shall we take a break for a quick tea dance?"
The hedgehog just sighs, "I don't stand a chance!"

In this sylvan dream where the laughter is loud,
Even the shy ones have drawn quite a crowd.
So join us in folly, forget all your woes,
In the tallest of grasses, let friendship grow close!

Hideaway of Green Hues

Lost in a realm of emerald delight,
A badger is wearing a hat that's too tight.
The bumblebees buzz with a tune so sweet,
While the trees sway to the rhythm of feet.

A picnic is planned with peanuts and jam,
But the raccoon sneaks off with the whole picnic clam.
As laughter erupts from the bushes nearby,
A fox cracks a joke – oh my, how we cry!

The worms have a meeting, it's top secret stuff,
While the birds toss their heads, saying, "That's rough!"
With caterpillars snickering, and crickets in glee,
This hideaway's charm is too grand for a spree!

So come revel in chaos, can't you tell?
In this realm of hues, everything's swell!
The giggles fly high like a kite on a breeze,
And here in the greenery, we laugh as we please.

Conversations in the Thicket

In the thick of the leaves, where the shadows play,
Frogs are discussing their grand leap all day.
The rabbits chime in with their tales of the night,
While the fireflies twinkle, a sparkling sight.

"Did you hear the one 'bout the bird in a hat?"
Exclaimed a wise owl, perched close to a rat.
The jokes that they share, oh, they crack up in fits,
As the hedgehog throws pies, aiming mostly for bits.

A turtle with sunglasses sips lemonade slow,
While a couple of mice juggle breadcrumbs in tow.
"I once caught a fish this big!" yells a squirrel,
But the tail's just a twig, oh how it did whirl!

In this talkative thicket where nonsense reigns high,
Every critter's a comedian, oh my! Oh my!
With laughter that echoes through branches and leaves,
We share in this banter, a joy that never leaves.

Raindrops on a Canopy

As raindrops come tapping a rhythmic soft tune,
The squirrels take cover and party like loons.
A puddle's a dance floor for frogs in their best,
While the chipmunks all twirl, putting moves to the test.

Beneath the wet leaves, a chatty duck quacks,
"Why don't we join in? There's no need for slack!"
With splashes galore and a giggle or two,
A whirlwind of water, oh, how they all flew!

The clouds take a bow, as the sun peeks out shy,
"Let's dry off and frolic!" suggests a wise fly.
But the beetles are stuck in their raindrop debate,
"What's better, a drizzle or a splashy fate?"

So gather your buddies beneath the sky's glow,
Let's laugh through the raindrops, let laughter flow slow.
For in this delight of the storm's funny grace,
We find all our joy in this wet, happy place!

Evergreen Sanctuary

In the shade of leafy cheer,
A squirrel pretends to steer.
A raccoon dons a bowtie neat,
While ants march on with tiny feet.

Beneath the branches, laughter swells,
As chipmunks spin their funny tales.
A frog croaks out a silly tune,
While grasshoppers dance, making a swoon.

The breeze whispers of playful jest,
As rabbits in their suits feel blessed.
They juggle acorns, what a sight!
Who knew trees could ignite such delight?

In this haven, joy takes flight,
With critters busting moves day and night.
The sky an artist's playful brush,
Creating giggles in the lush.

Tranquil Moments in Leafy Enclosures

In a leafy nook, the bees conspire,
To tickle flowers and never tire.
A caterpillar does ballet,
While twirling leaves just laugh away.

A tortoise thinks he's quick and spry,
But sees the snail and wonders why.
They race beneath the fronding trees,
Imagining they float on breeze.

Geese play chess with tiny pawns,
As dandelions blow, dreamt upon.
The ladybugs share gossip too,
"Have you heard what the lilies grew?"

Sunlight spills like laughter bright,
Wrapping all in delight's light.
In this grove, mirth reigns supreme,
With every rustle, a wandering dream.

Echoes of Nature in Green Hues

In the emerald halls where humor thrives,
Laughter echoes, waking lives.
A wise old owl cracks a joke,
While playfully stalking a sleepy cloak.

The thorns chuckle with rosy grace,
While mushrooms play a hiding place.
A beaver bobs with a croaky cheer,
Saying, "Life's a dam, but I persevere!"

The butterflies roll with giggles bright,
Chasing sunlight from morning till night.
A bumblebee hums a silly song,
In this green stage where all belong.

Mirth dances lightly on the breeze,
Bringing joy beneath the trees.
In every rustle, a silent shout,
Nature's laughter spreading about.

Where the Green World Meets the Sky

A frog in a tie jumps with flair,
He struts like a king without a care.
The clouds play peek-a-boo, oh what a sight,
While worms spin dreams of a dance at night.

Buzzing bees wear tiny hats,
As ladybugs plan their acrobatic acts.
The trees chuckle softly, swaying free,
While squirrels debate on tea and spree.

A picnic blanket sways in delight,
As ants rehearse a grand ballet tonight.
Beneath the branches, laughter does spill,
In nature's laughter, we find our thrill.

The sun winks down with a golden grin,
While grass tickles toes where joys begin.
In this jolly realm where shadows play,
Life dances by in a humorous ballet.

Encased in Nature's Closet

In the wardrobe of trees, all stocked with cheer,
A squirrel dons socks, thinks fashion is near.
Ferns flaunt their frills like a runway star,
As bumblebees buzz, dashing from afar.

The roots gossip softly, a secretive chat,
While mushrooms debate who's the fanciest hat.
"I'm spongy and cute!" one puffs with glee,
"I'm the life of the party, just wait and see!"

Lizards lounge in the cozy embrace,
Sharing wild tales in this leafy place.
And crickets compose songs, cheeky and bright,
While the sun plays peek-a-boo, what a delight!

The branches giggle in a breezy swirl,
As butterflies dance their colorful whirl.
Inside this closet where wonders bloom,
Nature's playful spirit fills every room.

The Peace of Leafy Stillness

In the quiet where whispers tickle the air,
A snail plays slow, without a care.
The leaves sway gently, a rustling sigh,
As a hedgehog rolls by, oh me, oh my!

The pond reflects dreams in dreamy hues,
While ducks quack gossip about the news.
A turtle debates if now is the time,
To join in the fun or continue to climb.

Mice hold a conference in soft, grassy beds,
Discussing the merits of cheese and breads.
Above, a crow calls with a raucous cheer,
"Join me for mischief! The coast is clear!"

In this leafy stillness where giggles are found,
Laughter floats lightly, all around.
Every moment a treasure, uniquely spun,
In the peace of green, life's just begun.

Elysium Beneath the Foliage

In the haven concealed from the sun's bright eye,
A rabbit wearing glasses wonders why.
An owl sips tea from a dandelion cup,
While chipmunks gossip, all huddled up.

The clovers giggle, they've secrets to share,
While ladybugs mingle without a care.
It's a carnival here beneath leafy realms,
Nature's antics run wild at the helms!

A swing made of vines swings to and fro,
As frogs on a log put on quite a show.
Squirrels are acrobats, leaping with flair,
In this playground of wonders, love's in the air.

With joy cascading like rain from the trees,
In Elysium's laughter, we dance with ease.
Amongst the green magic where fun holds sway,
Life finds a rhythm in a quirky way.

Secrets in the Leafy Haven

Amidst the branches, squirrels plot,
Why do they scurry? That's the thought!
They chat and chuckle, tails held high,
Creating mischief in the sky.

A rabbit hops, tripping on twigs,
Dancing in circles, oh how it wig!
With each little leap, a giggle is shared,
In this leafy place, joy is declared.

A snail slips slow, with a wink and a grin,
Racing the beetle, bound to win!
But oh, what folly, they're both outpaced,
In a hide-and-seek game, perfectly misplaced.

So if you wander to this green brigade,
Just know the rules of their fun charade.
Keep your ears open for whispers of jest,
In this playful haven, you're truly blessed.

Shelter from the Sun's Gaze

A shady spot, where shadows play,
Where ants march in a line, hooray!
With a picnic basket full of treats,
A feast of crumbs, oh what delights!

The little ones giggle, flying kites,
While butterflies join in on their flights.
A squirrel drops acorns, causing a rain,
And laughter erupts, both wild and insane.

A hot dog rolls, chased by a bee,
The sun's too bright; who could disagree?
They dodge and weave, beneath the shade,
In this sunny mess, new games are made.

So come, take refuge from the blaze,
In shade-filled antics and sunny malaise.
A world of fun, just step inside,
And let the laughter be your guide.

The Verdant Refuge

Leaves a rustle, secrets swirl,
In this spot, let imaginations unfurl.
A raccoon wears a hat, quite absurd,
Claiming it's fashion, though it's unheard!

A worm does the twist with style so grand,
While a beat-up frog joins the band.
Croaking a tune that makes no sense,
Yet all the creatures bop, so intense!

Twirls and twirls in the grassy floor,
Tumbling critters, always wanting more.
From ants with hats to crickets that sing,
This vibrant refuge is a funny fling.

So join the party, don't be late,
Where laughter grows in leafy fate.
In this lounge of green, you might just find,
A chuckle or two to ease your mind!

Shadows of Lush Serenity

In the cool shade, a cat naps tight,
Dreaming of fish with all its might.
But a bird swoops down, oh what a tease,
"Catch me if you can!"—cat stirs with unease.

The sun tries hard, but shadows win,
A tickling breeze makes the creature grin.
Beneath the leaves, where giggles flow,
Nature's joke is the grandest show.

Patchy sunlight through emerald beams,
Splits the day into giggly dreams.
A dragonfly hitches a ride on a dog,
Creating chaos—a comedic fog!

Join this gathering, don't be shy,
With creatures laughing beneath the sky.
In shadows' arms, find quirky glee,
A silly world, just for you and me.

Dreaming in the Leafy Shade

A squirrel danced upon the vine,
While bees took turns sipping the wine.
A frog complained, 'Where's my chair?'
As crickets tuned their evening prayer.

The shadows played a little game,
With whispers that just felt the same.
A butterfly lost track of time,
While ants perfected their silly rhyme.

A picnic spread with quirky flair,
With sandwiches shaped like teddy bears.
The sunlight winked as laughter spread,
And all the world was joy instead.

The Garden's Hidden Shelter

In the garden, laughter grows,
Where carrots wear their fanciest clothes.
Tomatoes giggle, red and round,
As onions join the funny sound.

A hedgehog pranced in polka dots,
Chasing after the dancing pots.
While bumblebees held court at tea,
Announcing that broccoli's free!

The flowers wore the craziest hats,
While worms organized their loose strands of mats.
The breeze hummed beats from far-off lands,
And earthworms staged their little bands.

Fern-cloaked Whispers

Beneath the ferns, the shadows shone,
A gnome rolled dice on a mushroom throne.
The toadstool tapped its tiny feet,
While snails formed a choral retreat.

Laughter bubbled from the brook,
Where frogs held cook-offs with a look.
A parrot squawked the silliest joke,
As yonder trees began to poke.

The leaves, in fits, began to sway,
As squirrels cheered the antics at play.
A ladybug wore a crown of dew,
And danced with joy for all she knew.

A Mellow Shade of Joy

In the warm glow of dappled rays,
I caught a snail in a slow-paced haze.
A lazy cat planned its grand escape,
While the daisies surveyed the landscape.

With cotton candy clouds above,
And cheeky squirrels in the grove,
A pillow fight with fluffy leaves,
Brought giggles from the big oak trees.

The grass tickled my toes, oh dear,
As bees buzzed near, quite insincere.
Then came a breeze, a gusty laugh,
And all my worries took a bath.

Harmony Within Nature's Caress

When squirrels dance like tiny clowns,
And birds wear crowns of leafy frowns,
The flowers giggle in the breeze,
Nature hums her tunes with ease.

A frog jumps high, an acrobat,
While bees debate on where they're at,
The sun peeks through with playful rays,
While butterflies steal sunny days.

Ducks quack jokes by the pond's edge,
As rabbits hop beyond the hedge,
Laughing leaves are swaying low,
In this green world, joy will flow.

Together we'll share nature's cheer,
With every laugh, the world draws near,
In this bright dance where we belong,
A song of fun, forever strong.

Emerald Echoes in Stillness

In a patch of grass, a picnic waits,
With sandwiches and silly plates,
A chipmunk eyes the cake with glee,
As ants scheme plans for a big spree.

A breeze brings whispers, soft and light,
While ladybugs take off in flight,
The ticklish blades tease our bare toes,
And giggles swell in nature's prose.

A raccoon peeks with curious eyes,
Searching for snacks, oh what a surprise!
With fruit in hand, we share a laugh,
While the sun throws gold in the path.

Bubbles float like dreams divine,
In this green patch, all is fine,
With every laugh, the moments cling,
Beneath the trees, we laugh and sing.

Where Shade Meets Serenity

In a cozy nook of leafy shade,
We play charades, plans are made,
The sun throws sparkles on our heads,
As squirrels exchange their silly threads.

With each rustle, a tickling sound,
In this sanctuary, joy is found,
A turtle strolls with fashion flair,
While grasshoppers leap in mid-air.

We sip our drinks with silly straws,
Sharing secrets and little flaws,
A butterfly winks, oh so sly,
As clouds drift by, painted in pie.

With laughter ringing through the trees,
Wind whispers softly, "Do as you please,"
In this tranquil and happy place,
Nature's laughter wears a bright face.

The Canopy's Embrace

Beneath the branches, giggles rise,
As squirrels plot with tiny spies,
We toss a ball; it sails so high,
While clouds are grinning in the sky.

A funny hedgehog joins our fun,
With prickly puns; he's never done,
We crown him king of leafy games,
With laughter echoing our names.

The brook joins in with a chuckle low,
As fish leap out, putting on a show,
A duck quacks jokes, his timing tight,
In this wild world, all feels right.

Laughter dances, spins, and twirls,
Amongst the ferns and nature's pearls,
In the embrace of the lush and bold,
These silly tales will never grow old.

The Kaleidoscope of Leaves

In a swirling dance of hues,
Leaves tickle noses, what a ruse!
A squirrel prances, does a jig,
While a beetle tries to wiggle big.

Frogs in chorus, croak out tunes,
While dancing with the playful loons.
Twirling tops and whirling games,
Nature's laughter knows no names.

Rain taps lightly on the ground,
Dancing droplets, joy unbound.
A jester to the passing breeze,
Whispers of joy rustle through trees.

So come and join the leafy spree,
Where giggles grow on every tree.
In this place of vibrant glee,
Nature's clown plays endlessly.

Oasis of the Whispering Breeze

A gust of wind, a playful sigh,
Tugging hats as clouds float by.
The daisies laugh, they cannot hide,
While giggling grasshoppers leap and glide.

Breezes carry secrets, oh so sweet,
Like whispers bouncing from tree to feet.
They tease the leaves, they shout and play,
While ants march by, all work and sway.

The sun peeks down with a cheeky grin,
Glimmers dancing on a leaf-like skin.
While frogs, in chorus, croak their glee,
Echoing joy, from tree to spree.

A patchwork quilt of light and shade,
Where laughter and fun never fade.
In this oasis of breezy fun,
Life's but a game, in the warmth of the sun.

Reveries in the Green Light

A sprinkle of sunlight, a dash of cheer,
The bushes chuckle, the laughter is near.
Chasing shadows, ducking a tree,
Bouncing along, wild and free.

A tumbleweed rolls, wearing a hat,
Sassy little critters engage in chat.
Around the bend, a frog leaps high,
High fives with birds flying by.

A breeze stirs softly, tickling noses,
While ants in a line march for poses.
Nature's party, all invited,
In the green light, hearts delighted.

Wrap me in laughter, joy, and glee,
This whimsical world is the place to be.
In rev'res of green, we're all aligned,
Let's dance in the light, leaving worries behind.

Shelter of the Whispering Woods

In the woods where whispers dwell,
Trees spin tales, the stories swell.
Squirrels gossip in playful jest,
As shadows dance, we are blessed.

The greens abound, a quirky sight,
A wiggling snail, oh what a fright!
While branches sway, the breezes tease,
Laughter grows among the leaves.

Tickling toes and sneaking peeks,
A chorus of nature gently speaks.
In every nook, there's joy to find,
Adventures woven, sweetly twined.

So let's embark on this silly trek,
A whimsical ride, what the heck!
In the sheltering woods, we'll roam,
With laughter echoing, we find our home.

Nature's Gentle Swaddle

In a blanket of leaves, we lay,
Laughing as the squirrels play.
The sunlight weaves through the trees,
Tickling us like a warm breeze.

A parrot scolds a sleepy cat,
While a raccoon tips its hat.
Butterflies dance, a funny sight,
In nature's laughter, pure delight.

A shy snail slips on a leaf,
Exclaiming, "This is beyond belief!"
The flowers gossip in soft tones,
While ants march by with tiny phones.

We giggle at the buzzing bees,
Wearing hats made out of leaves.
In this world, so full of cheer,
Nature's swaddle keeps us near.

Refuge Amongst the Verdure

In emerald shadows, we collide,
Finding joy where mischief hides.
A frog croaks tunes so out of tune,
While lizards claim the afternoon.

A chipmunk sneaks some tasty snacks,
Wearing his best of fashion hacks.
Each flower blooms with laughter loud,
In this green shelter, we feel proud.

The breeze whispers tales of fun,
As we chase shadows 'til we're done.
Mice in hats and shoes parade,
In this wild, delightful escapade.

A rainbow forms from morning dew,
Painting smiles in every hue.
Amongst the greens, we yell and sing,
Nature's refuge is a silly thing.

The Tranquil Grove's Serenade

A sleepy bear plays hide and seek,
While we giggle, feeling cheeky.
A dancing leaf twirls in the air,
As if the wind has no care.

A hedgehog dons a tiny crown,
Wandering through its leafy town.
It tips its hat, quite full of cheer,
Making us laugh, "Oh dear, oh dear!"

The breeze carries a chorus bold,
As stories of the forest unfold.
There's laughter hiding in each nook,
Every branch, a funny book.

An owl hoots, an unfunny clown,
As squirrels tease him up and down.
In this serene, whimsical space,
Nature giggles, oh what a place!

Dreams in the Dappled Light

In beams that dance upon the ground,
Funny shadows twist around.
A fox in socks prances near,
Wiggling its tail without a fear.

The mushrooms hold a dance-off grand,
As beetles join a little band.
They croon sweet tunes to every bug,
While the daisies dance, oh so snug!

A butterfly with polka dots,
Flutters by, quite happy in spots.
Dreams weave in this golden glow,
As nature's antics put on a show.

We chase the light, a playful feat,
As crickets chirp in rapid beat.
In this dappled dream, we declare,
Laughter blooms in the sweet, warm air.

The Cove of Soft Breezes

In a cove where giggles play,
Winds toss hats on silly days.
A sandwich flies, it's quite absurd,
The seagulls chuckle, oh the word!

Lemonade spills, what a sight,
On sunburned noses, glowing bright.
The waves dance with a shiny glee,
A crab waves back, it's glad to see!

Under the shade, a cat naps wide,
While turtles race, but none can glide.
Fins flapping, here comes a friend,
A fishy tale with no clear end!

As laughter lifts like a balloon,
We sing to the rhythm of the tune.
In this cove of mirth and cheer,
Every moment sparkles here!

Enchanted by Emerald Light

In emerald glow, the frogs do croak,
Each ribbit sounds like a funny joke.
They dance on lilypads, quite the scene,
While dragonflies wear crowns of green!

A squirrel in shades jumps for a snack,
Finding acorns while doing a backtrack.
Laughing loudly, he drops his prize,
A nut rolls fast, to everyone's surprise!

Dancing bees in a dizzy delight,
Chasing shadows, buzzing feels right.
A pixie sneezes, off goes a shoe,
And everyone giggles—oh, what a view!

The sun chuckles, casting odd shapes,
And weaved in magic, here comes a tape.
A concert starts, crickets in line,
With every tune, we laugh and dine!

Beneath the Boughs of Tranquility

Beneath the boughs where whispers dwell,
A rabbit tells stories, oh so swell.
With floppy ears and sideway glance,
He spins tall tales that make us prance!

In the vines, a snail takes his trip,
Slower than laughter, he makes a quip.
"Why rush," he says, "when there's so much time?
I'll have my tea and savor the rhyme!"

The flowers giggle, tickled by bees,
As a grasshopper hops with utmost ease.
A tumbleweed rolls just for fun,
Chasing a shadow, away it runs!

As twilight peeks through leafy gowns,
Laughter echoes, and no one frowns.
Here beneath boughs, joy takes its flight,
Where silly moments turn day to night!

The Arbor's Secret Words

In the arbor where secrets confide,
Whispers of joy take a playful ride.
A parrot spills tales of wiggly worms,
While squirrels argue over acorn terms!

An old owl hoots with a crooked grin,
"Why do they argue? Let's just begin!"
He opens a book with pages so bright,
And reads with flair, a comical plight!

The wind carries laughter like a friend,
Cracking jokes that seem to bend.
"Why did the twig break?" they holler in glee,
"Because it couldn't find a leaf to agree!"

In the trees, mischief is never far,
With giggles and jests, we raise the bar.
The arbor echoes, each secret unfurled,
A symphony of humor in a leafy world!

A Nest of Nature's Tapestry

Leaves play hide and seek with the breeze,
Squirrels gossip about acorns with ease.
A bird tries to sing, but forgets the tune,
While bugs dance around, making merry by noon.

The sun peeks through like a shy little mouse,
As shadows twist around, filling the house.
A rabbit pops out, with a curious glance,
In this vibrant green, they all seem to prance.

A butterfly flits, with a wink and a nod,
Near a flower that laughs, "I'm the fairest of clod!"
Nature's own circus, with laughter and cheer,
Where every small creature feels perfectly dear.

So gather your friends, let the fun be the goal,
In this tapestry garden, we're all on a roll.
With giggles and grins, as bright as can be,
A nest of pure joy, just so wild and free.

Where Shadows Dance in Green

In a patch of shade, where the giggles play,
A cat with a hat dreams the afternoon away.
A frog in a tux takes a leap with flair,
While ants march by, completely unaware.

Beneath leafy arches where sunlight cracks bright,
The fireflies twinkle, as if taking flight.
A snail with a plan says, "I'll race you all!"
But they just slow down when they hear the call.

The breeze shares secrets, you'll never believe,
Of the garden's antics on this fine autumn eve.
A picnic of laughter, with crumbs on the grass,
Where each silly story earns another loud laugh.

So come take a peek, where shadows play tricks,
And the world is awash with whimsical picks.
Every green corner's a stage for delight,
In this theater of fun, life feels so just right.

The Lush Oasis of Solace

In a jungle of chuckles, where wild things are found,
An octopus juggles, just spinning around.
The parakeets gossip about the best seats,
While a turtle claims victory in slow-motion feats.

A monkey with style swings high from a vine,
Sipping on nectar, feeling just fine.
With laughter that echoes, the trees join the cheer,
In this oasis of giggles, it's all crystal clear.

Mushrooms wear hats, oh what a delight,
They dance in the moonlight, keeping spirits light.
A chorus of critters sings songs of the day,
In a lush, green paradise, come frolic and play!

So let's gather 'round, in this haven so nice,
Where every moment's a slice of sweet spice.
With friends all around, and joy in the air,
This oasis of solace is beyond compare.

Chasing Sunbeams through Leaves

With giggles and wiggles, we dash through the trees,
In a game of tag played by bustling bees.
The sunlight cascades in a warm, golden hue,
While grasshoppers cheer, saying, "We see you!"

A puppy named Max hops, chasing a friend,
A squirrel with style, who just won't pretend.
They leap through the air, sparks flying with glee,
It's a festival frolic, as wild as can be!

The leaves whisper stories of legends so grand,
Of the mischief and joy from this playful band.
A fairytale scene, with laughter in the air,
Where even the trees wear expressions of care.

So come take a stroll, let your worries just slide,
In this sunbeam chase, there's no reason to hide.
Embrace all the winks that the sunlight bestows,
In a world made of smiles, where the fun always flows.

Dreaming in a Leafy Refuge

In a nook where shadows play,
Squirrels dance, they're here to stay.
A young rabbit on a spree,
Chasing dreams of carrots, wee!

Sunbeams flicker, light the scene,
As ants march in a line, so keen.
A ladybug wears polka dots,
While frogs croak out their cheerful plots.

The breeze whispers silly tales,
Of turtles who go speedier than snails.
With each gust, the laughter flows,
Even grumpy owls crack grins, who knows?

In this haven, cheeks all round,
Nature's giggles all abound.
Underneath the leafy sway,
Life's a game, come out and play!

The Serenity of Leafy Enclosure

A gopher hums a charming song,
While vines weave stories, never wrong.
Tails of foxes flick like flags,
Dreaming dreams in grassy jags.

Beneath the boughs, a picnic spreads,
With sandwiches and funny spreads.
Flies compete for tater chips,
While bees do dance and perform flips.

Chirpy birds join squeaky vows,
Telling jokes to laughing cows.
Time ticks by, yet seems so slow,
In this paradise where chuckles flow.

And as the sun begins to dip,
Bugs throw a nighttime poetry trip.
Under the twinkling starry glow,
The leafy stage steals every show!

Pause in the Embrace of Nature

A chubby chipmunk might just sing,
As butterflies start their circus fling.
The grass tickles toes with a laugh,
Inviting all to join the craft.

A pebble whispers secrets bold,
To the little snails, tales of old.
"Life is gooey, don't you see?
Slow is fine; just let it be!"

Laughter echoes, a joyful ring,
As noisy crickets play and fling.
The tree trunks tap a silly beat,
Together, all dance on tiny feet!

Moments stretch, in this jolly lair,
Life's hilarious, just take a care.
With mischief woven in each leaf,
The forest spins in gleeful grief!

Lullabies Beneath the Green Canopy

Under sighing branches low,
Little critters start their show.
The shadows waltz, they clap and cheer,
For the night has come near!

Toadstools host a vibrant night,
As fireflies chase with flickering light.
Each glow a giggle, bright and fair,
While owls join in with a crooning air.

The moon grins wide, a cheeky chap,
As hedgehogs settle for a nap.
Dreams fluff around like dandelion seeds,
Sprouting laughter, that's all one needs!

In beds of moss, soft and round,
Nature's lullabies all around.
With every rustle, a chuckle shared,
The spirit of joy is truly bared!

Conversations among the Branches

Two squirrels debate, who's the best chef,
While birds chirp their tunes, oh what a mess!
A leaf jokes aloud, 'You've burnt my lunch!'
Laughter erupts, as they all take the plunge.

A breeze joins the fray, tickling their toes,
'You think you can dance? Well, here's how it goes!'
They spin and they twirl, limbs flaying about,
The party is wild, there's nothing in doubt!

A wise old branch grumbles, 'What's all this fuss?'
'We're just having fun,' replies a cheeky muss!
With acorns as snacks, and pine cones for hats,
They toast to their antics, these jovial brats!

As sunbeams peek through, they all burst in cheer,
'This is the best day! Let's do it, my dear!'
With giggles and curls, under fronds they all lay,
In this wacky old world, they'll frolic away!

The Peace of the Green Cloak.

In a cozy embrace, where shadows collide,
A snail takes a nap, in a place to abide.
'Hey, move over here!' whispers a nearby leaf,
'You're blocking my sun!' fills the air with belief.

Ants march in formation, on a grand parade,
'We brought snacks for all, who wants lemonade?'
With tiny cups raised, the revelry flows,
They clink little shells, as laughter still grows.

A ladybug winks, as she spins on a vine,
A centipede chimes in, 'That move is divine!'
The branches they sway, in ecstasy's fight,
While overhead giggles weave through the light.

Nestled in comfort, beneath leaves galore,
They share all their secrets and so much more.
With a wink and a nod, the day drifts along,
In the peace of the cloak, they all sing their song!

Whispers Beneath the Canopy

Crickets sing softly, above, what a tune!
While worms in the soil are plotting by noon.
'Have you heard the news?' chirps a gopher with glee,
'The raindrops will dance; oh, just wait and see!'

A wise old owl hoots, 'I've seen it all here,
From birds with bad jokes to frogs full of cheer.'
The mushrooms all giggle, as shadows converge,
In this hallowed patch where giggles emerge.

'Let's make a new game,' calls a bouncy young sprout,
'Who can grow tallest, without any doubt?'
They stretch and they sway, all in friendly jest,
While the beetles nearby cheer on with zest.

As the moonlight kisses the world with its charm,
They settle their bets, and all bask in calm.
With whispers and warmth, they revel, they play,
In this patch of delight, together they stay!

Emerald Shade Embrace

In a forest so lush, where shadows convene,
The creatures hold court, in this verdant scene.
A bear with a bowtie debates on his class,
'What's proper food? Only flowers or grass?'

A rabbit insists, 'It's all set in stone,
Carrots are king, you can't eat alone!'
While a wise old fox rolls his eyes with a grin,
'Let's munch on our chats, that's where we begin!'

With the chipmunks as waiters, bringing snacks galore,
The laughter cascades, like leaves on the floor.
A caterpillar sports a tiny beret,
While crickets tap dance; they're here for a play!

As the sun dips low, casting shadows that sway,
They dance in a circle, till end of the day.
With emerald embrace, they gather 'round tight,
In the heart of their giggles, all feels so right!

The Hush of Nature's Blanket

In a cozy nook where laughter stirs,
A raccoon sings while a squirrel purrs.
Clouds look on, wearing a shady grin,
As birds crack jokes with a chirpy spin.

Beneath the boughs, a picnic awaits,
With sandwiches served on funky plates.
The ants throw a dance, so out of line,
While bees buzz along to the party's rhyme.

Leaves rustle softly, like whispers shared,
As woodland critters join, unprepared.
An owl squawks loudly, "What's the fuss?"
To squirrels debating who's first on the bus!

So here we lounge beneath the sway,
With Mother Nature as our cabaret.
Tickles of sunlight, funny and bright,
In this leafy realm, all feels just right.

A Retreat among Leafy Giants

A hedgehog dons a tiny cap,
Napoleon's dream falls into a nap.
Nearby, a snail plays chess with a bug,
While mushrooms spark a growing drug.

Big trees gossip, their branches intertwined,
As curious critters come to unwind.
A chipmunk juggles acorns with flair,
As laughter bounces in the cool air.

The flowers bloom in riotous hues,
Each petal chimes with cheeky views.
With giggles and wiggles, the night creatures creep,
Chasing fireflies while the world's asleep.

In this green retreat, joy takes the lead,
Where every leaf is a place to succeed.
So let's raise a toast with twigs as our straws,
To the wild and the wacky, with nature's applause!

Echoes Beneath the Fruiting Boughs

Beneath layers of leaves, the fun's ablaze,
Tucked in the branches where apples gaze.
Cherries giggle, tickling the breeze,
While plums tell jokes, fit to tease.

A squirrel rode in on a grape's wild train,
Singing songs of sunshine, dancing in the rain.
They compete in a race, who's the fastest flyer?
The winner grabs a slice of pie on fire!

Grasshoppers try to tap dance in tune,
While others lounge under the bright full moon.
"Hey, look at that crow, trying to croon!
I think he's got some humor in his swoon!"

In this canopy of giggle and glee,
Every critter lends a hand, you see.
Beneath these boughs, laughter reigns supreme,
In a world of fun, we happily dream.

Serenity in the Forest's Heart

In the forest's arm, where whispers play,
A fox wears spectacles, smartly gay.
Meanwhile, a turtle rolls in the grass,
Saying, "Life's a journey; let's make it a blast!"

A rabbit recounts tales, silly and bold,
Of feats so epic, they're already old.
"Remember last spring when I leaped a mile?
My ears flew off; now every dog wears my style!"

With dappled light dancing, the scene's a delight,
As chipmunks applaud the forest's great height.
The trees hold secrets in every crack,
While shadows gamble on the leafy track.

So nestle right here in this whimsical nook,
Where stories are spun and cakes barely cook.
Amidst the green, let laughter dispense,
In the forest's heart, we find our existence!

The Quiet Refuge of Leaves

In the realm of leafy giggles,
Squirrels make a fuss,
Chasing shadows and each other,
Who knew trees could cuss?

Beneath the branches' canopy,
A picnic takes its place,
Ants march in a line, you see,
Looking like a race!

Frisbees fly through lacy air,
Dodging branches sharp and spry,
Laughter spills without a care,
As leaves dance on by.

With a blanket spread in glee,
And snacks placed just so right,
We share our joy quite merrily,
In nature's delight.

Beneath the Whispering Boughs

A hedgehog sports a tiny hat,
He winks from bark-lined dives,
While chatty birds form a format,
To tell their tales of lives.

The breeze joins in, it sings along,
Tickling leaves and roots,
While squirrels practice acrobatics,
In the midst of fruit dispute.

With sandwiches and juice so sweet,
We giggle at the sight,
As a raccoon scampers on fleet,
Daring us to a fight!

Who knew such fun could be found,
In this shady paradise?
Laughter here is quite profound,
With mischief that's precise.

The Shade of Sylvan Dreams

Twirling leaves in playful flight,
Dare to float, then glide,
While rabbits hop with pure delight,
In this leafy hide.

A gopher pulls a prank or two,
As we munch our snacks,
He pops up with a view askew,
How joyfully he cracks!

The butterflies put on a show,
With colors bright and bold,
They twirl and dance, all in a row,
Our laughter takes a hold.

Underneath this leafy dome,
We share our little jokes,
In this nature-fueled home,
Where happiness provokes.

Beneath Verdant Skies

Bubbles float and giggles rise,
As kids run without care,
Caught in clouds of sunny lies,
Life's a game we share.

A pair of frogs in concert sing,
Their croaks a funny tune,
While turtles plot the next big thing,
To hide away by noon.

With picnics spread on grassy hills,
Where ants can join the feast,
We share our laughs and simple thrills,
With joy that never ceased.

Wandering through this leafy maze,
We find a world of cheer,
And dance along to nature's ways,
With friends that always near.

Solace Found in Green Shadow

In the shade of vibrant leaves,
Lizards dance and sunshine weaves.
Sipping tea from a plastic cup,
Hoping squirrels don't interrupt.

A friendly breeze begins to tease,
It rustles branches with such ease.
My sandwich flies, a seagull's prize,
While I just laugh 'neath leafy skies.

Picnic ants with grand designs,
Plotting routes, they draw the lines.
I wave goodbye to crumbs galore,
Their feast begins, my snack is no more.

In shadows deep the laughter rolls,
As nature's circus takes its tolls.
With every bite, a squirrel jumps,
And life is just one funny lump.

Green Veil of Repose

Beneath a cloak of leafy green,
I spot a bug that's quite obscene.
It dances 'round, a little mime,
While I just sip on old red wine.

A rabbit hops, he thinks he's sly,
While I, with snacks, just watch him spy.
He nibbles grass, I munch on cheese,
And giggle at his subtle tease.

The gnomes around, they're in a fight,
A battle with the ants tonight.
A moth drifts in, what a jest,
While I just slouch and take my rest.

The sun dips low, the shadows creep,
As dragonflies begin to leap.
With laughter rich and antics bold,
A tale of warmth and joy unfolds.

Beyond the Leafy Facade

A turtle struts, he thinks he's fast,
While I simply enjoy my snack blast.
He glances left, he glances right,
Then trips and tumbles—a comical sight.

Birds compose a chirpy tune,
As bees buzz by, immune to ruin.
A boisterous frog croaks loud and clear,
Announcing, "This is my domain, my dear!"

The sun is bright, the grass is soft,
While I spot squirrels acting aloof.
They plot and scheme with funny flair,
Who knew nature had so much to share?

And as the dusk begins to paint,
The trees become a giggling saint.
For laughter grows in every nook,
A curious tale, in time, we'll look.

In the Embrace of Nature's Green

A caterpillar takes a stroll,
With swagger that is quite the goal.
He flashes by, all smooth and keen,
While I just sip on lime ice cream.

The clouds above form silly shapes,
A dragon, horse, and well-dressed apes.
The shadows play a game of tag,
As I sit still, my thoughts do lag.

The chipmunks plot in secret rows,
While I just chuckle at their woes.
They scurry fast, but take a break,
And munch on nuts beside the lake.

In merry green, I find my cheer,
With nature's antics ever near.
Life's a jest, a joyous spree,
In shadows wrapped, just laugh with me!

Chill in the Whisper of Leaves

In a shady nook where laughter grows,
We chuckle at squirrels and silly crows.
The breeze tells jokes, the sun plays shy,
While ants hold parties, oh my, oh my!

With snacks on the grass, we jive and sway,
Dancing on picnics, come join the fray.
Bees buzz along with a comedic hum,
Who knew nature had such a sense of fun?

Giggling trees sway to the sound of our glee,
Wishing to join in, they rustle a plea.
The clouds float by, wearing silly hats,
Even the flowers laugh at the chitchats.

At sunset's call, we make quite a scene,
Chasing shadows, like kids, oh so keen.
Leaves fall like confetti, all joyous and bright,
In this wild, funny kingdom, we dance till the night!

Symphony of Silence Under Foliage

A chorus of whispers floats by on the air,
Crickets play violins without a care.
The rustling leaves join in with a tune,
While frogs croak solo beneath the moon.

Ducks quack harmony, marching in line,
They waddle along, acting divine.
Meanwhile, a rabbit beats on a drum,
To the rhythm of nature, oh what fun!

The deer sway gently, moving with grace,
While the turtles groove at a very slow pace.
The stars above blink in time to the beat,
With laughter and song, who can resist this sweet?

In our leafy hall, we share the stage,
As fireflies dance like a playful mage.
A lull in our laughter, the night wraps tight,
In this symphony, we blend with delight!

Eden of the Gentle Breeze

In a nook of laughter where daisies play,
The breeze brings secrets in a whimsical way.
We chase butterflies, falling on grass,
As giggles and laughter spring up en masse.

Clouds roll by in a wobbly line,
They tease the Sun, pointing, 'You're just fine!'
With ticklish winds that tug our hair,
Every moment's a gift, caught unaware.

A picnic deems all ants as the guests,
While gnats take turns in their wild, crazy quests.
Bumbling bees buzz with a curious cheer,
Claiming our sandwiches, "We're no volunteers!"

With the sun now sinking, shadows start to play,
And laughter fills the air, chasing worries away.
In this Eden, where joy sings anew,
We hold on to moments, too precious to rue!

Hiding in Nature's Embrace

Crouched by the bushes, we giggle with glee,
Squirrels play tag, how funny to see!
The sun peeks out, a curious friend,
Nature laughs softly, no need to pretend.

The brook gently babbles secretive pranks,
As fish flip and flounder, giving us thanks.
Each rustle above gives us quite a start,
What's that? A deer? Or just nature's art?

We hide in the foliage, chuckling with joy,
Imagining the tales of each critter and boy.
The wind whispers stories of laughter and cheer,
In this playful green world, let's disappear!

As twilight descends, shadows dance and glide,
Amongst trees so tall, secrets can hide.
We exit with smiles, hearts light as a feather,
Hiding in nature, oh, what lovely weather!

A Journey Through Verdant Shadows

In a jungle of leaves, I trip and fall,
Around me, the critters laugh one and all.
The squirrels throw acorns, oh what a sight,
As I dance with a tree, in the fading light.

I wear a hat made of twigs and grass,
Singing off-key, letting good times pass.
The shadows are friendly, they whisper to me,
Join the forest's party, just sing like a bee.

Branches hang low, like old pals at play,
Tickling my thoughts in a leafy ballet.
I tumble through ferns, with giggles galore,
The nature's my stage, and I'm always wanting more.

With vines for a belt, I stomp with delight,
These woods are alive, what a whimsical sight!
Beneath the broad boughs, I know I belong,
In the verdant shadows, life feels like a song.

The Safety of Leafy Wings

A parade of butterflies flutters on by,
Wearing hats made of petals, oh my, oh my!
They tease the grumpy old toad by the creek,
While I trip on a root, my balance is weak.

Under big leafy wings, all fears disappear,
The trees crack some jokes that only they hear.
The wind whispers secrets, tickles my nose,
I startle a rabbit, in my funny pose.

Frogs croak the chorus, the crickets provide,
A melody sweet where no worries can hide.
Even the rocks start to giggle and sway,
In this leafy abode, we all laugh and play.

So here on the ground, tucked beneath the green,
Life feels like a dance, a joyous routine.
With nature's embrace, there's nothing to fear,
The safety of wings makes laughter so dear.

Embraced by the Green Canopy

A breath of fresh air, I'm lost in the fun,
The trees are my pals, we laugh with the sun.
I join in their chatter, like leaves in the breeze,
Trying to balance while swatting at bees.

A squirrel starts juggling his prized acorn stash,
I'm clapping along, not a moment to clash.
We share a fine snack, a nut and a laugh,
While vines hug the air like a curious giraffe.

Ferns tickle my nose as I roll in the grass,
The leaves whisper tales of a long-gone class.
With every odd twist, I giggle and roll,
Embraced by the canopy, my heart feels whole.

So here, in this green, where the laughter grows,
Nature's silly antics brighten up the prose.
Who knew that such joy could sprout from a tree?
In this gentle embrace, just silly and free.

The Coolness of Nature's Heart

In the shade of the giants, I discover my stride,
With roots like my friends, we laugh side by side.
The breeze brings a chill that tickles my toes,
While daisies perform dances, in colorful clothes.

Whispers from willows draw me near the stream,
Where frogs play the banjo, fulfilling a dream.
Grasshoppers hop high, as giggles abound,
Nature's cool heart beats in laughter profound.

A parade of shadows leads my way through the trees,
Swaying with rhythm, just follow the breeze.
I chase after dandelions, fluffy and light,
In this cool, verdant world, everything feels right.

With giggles and grumbles, the wild's grown-up cheer,
Is all wrapped in green, laughter flowing clear.
The heart of the forest is blissfully bright,
In this playful haven, I dance with delight.

www.ingramcontent.com/pod-product-compliance
Lightning Source LLC
Chambersburg PA
CBHW070318120526
44590CB00017B/2728